PENCIL LETTER

Also by Irina Ratushinskaya

No, I'm Not Afraid (Bloodaxe Books, 1986)
Grey Is the Colour of Hope (Hodder & Stoughton, 1988)

IRINA RATUSHINSKAYA

Pencil Letter

ERIC BLOODAXE

BLOODAXE BOOKS

HUTCHINSON

London Melbourne Auckland Johannesburg

ISBN: 1 85224 049 0 hardback edition
       1 85224 050 4 paperback edition

First published 1988 by   ↶ ⟍
Bloodaxe Books Ltd,
P.O. Box 1SN, Newcastle upon Tyne NE99 1SN,
in the United Kingdom and Ireland,
and by Hutchinson Ltd,
an imprint of Century Hutchinson Ltd,
Brookmount House, 62-65 Chandos Place,
London WC2N 4NW,
overseas (excluding the USA) :
Century Hutchinson Australia Pty Ltd, P.O. Box 496,
16-22 Church Street, Hawthorn, Victoria 3122, Australia;
Century Hutchinson New Zealand Ltd,
P.O. Box 40-086, Glenfield, Auckland 10, New Zealand;
Century Hutchinson South Africa Pty Ltd,
P.O. Box 337, Bergvlei, 2012, South Africa.

                                  ! ⸱   325986

Bloodaxe Books Ltd acknowledges
the financial assistance of Northern Arts.

Typesetting by Tyneside Free Press Ltd,
Newcastle upon Tyne.

Printed in Great Britain by
Bell & Bain Limited, Glasgow, Scotland.

Translators

LC/SS	Lyn Coffin with Sergei Shishkoff
AK	Alyona Kojevnikov
DMcD	David McDuff
RMcK/HS	Richard McKane with Helen Szamuely
BM	Blake Morrison (assisted by Mark Frankland)
HS/RMcK	Helen Szamuely with Richard McKane
AM	Alan Myers
CR	Carol Rumens (assisted by Yurij Drobyshev)
DW	Daniel Weissbort

Thirteen of the translations by David McDuff were first published in *No, I'm Not Afraid* by Irina Ratushinskaya (Bloodaxe Books, 1986). Some of the translations by David McDuff and Alan Myers were broadcast in a *Living Poet* programme of Irina Ratushinskaya's work by BBC Radio 3 in 1987. Other translations have been published by Keston College, in the *Observer* and in *Poetry Review*.

Contents

Publisher's Note

Irina Ratushinskaya was arrested on 17 September 1982, and charged with 'anti-Soviet agitation and propaganda'. On 3 March 1983, one day before her 29th birthday, she was sentenced to seven years' hard labour in a 'strict regime' labour camp and five years' internal exile. Her crime: writing poetry.

The first poem in this book, 'Pencil Letter', was written in the KGB Prison in Kiev, in November 1982, as she waited for her trial. In April 1983, she was sent to a labour camp at Barashevo in Mordovia, three hundred miles south-east of Moscow. For over three years she was held prisoner there in the Small Zone, a special unit for women prisoners of conscience.

Some poems smuggled out of the Small Zone were included in *No, I'm Not Afraid* (Bloodaxe Books, 1986), and several of these – written between May 1983 and August 1984 – are reprinted here. This book then continues with the other poems Irina Ratushinskaya wrote in the camp between October 1984 and June 1986, and with some poems written in the KGB Prison in Kiev, where she was held for three months before finally being freed on 9 October 1986, on the eve of the Reykjavik summit. The book ends with poems written after her release, in Kiev and Moscow, before she left the Soviet Union for the West in December 1986.

Irina's own testament, *Grey Is the Colour of Hope* (Hodder & Stoughton, 1988), tells the full story of her imprisonment in the Small Zone, which included some spells in a punishment isolation cell, or SHIZO *(shtrafnoy izolyator)*, and some in the camp's internal prison, or PKT *(Pomescheniye Kamernogo Tipa)*, at Yavas. These initials are used in this book to indicate where, and under what conditions, particular poems were written.

Irina copied her poems in a tiny hand onto strips of paper which were hidden and then smuggled out of the camp. Some of these are reproduced (actual size) at the back of this book.

PENCIL LETTER

Pencil Letter

I know it won't be received
Or sent. The page will be
In shreds as soon as I have scribbled it.
Later. Sometime. You've grown used to it,
Reading between the lines that never reached you,
Understanding everything. On the tiny sheet,
Not making haste, I find room for the night.
What's the hurry, when the hour that's passed
Is all part of the same time, the same unknown term.
The word stirs under my hand
Like a starling, a rustle, a movement of eyelashes.
Everything's fine. But don't come into my dream yet.
In a little while I will tie my sadness into a knot,
Throw my head back and on my lips there'll be a seal,
A smile, my prince, although from afar.
Can you feel the warmth of my hand
Passing through your hair, over your hollow cheek.
December winds have blown on your face . . .
How thin you are . . . Stay in my dream.
Open the window. The pillow is hot.
Footsteps at the door, and a bell tolling in the tower:
Two, three . . . Remember, you and I never said
Goodbye. It doesn't matter.
Four o'clock . . . That's it. How heavily it tolls.

Night Song of the Tower

Win-ter. It's dark.
Close the win-dow.
Don't let in
The last light.
How many winters of grief
For all the summers.

Fourth dream –
And afterwards?
To choke a groan
With a handkerchief?
What century?
Ungifted calculation.
The snow is like bleach
And burns the eyes.
Breathe calmer!
Don't dare! Don't dare!

Oh, what a strange tower!
Nanny of my troubled nights,
How marvellous it would be to cry
On your shoulder in just my night shirt.
Classic bliss!
Can I let slip such an opportunity?
Yet I do. The sheet under my cheek
Bears a mark.
It is branded, so it can't be swiped,
The punishment cell, i.e. the KGB...
It's stifling. A lump in my throat.
Nanny, do you want me to tell
You an outdated story?
Listen old girl, stop grumbling.
Ignore the fact that the subject is hackneyed.
There's a cause for everything in this world.

Once upon a time there were some grey mice
Who lived in a metal trunk.
They tried get by in their corner
As quietly as possible.
They were fruitful and multiplied,
As the Lord ordered the wild beasts:
They would give birth on the quiet
And sing this song.

Song of the Mice

Sleep my little one,
My brave little mouse.
You'll sleep an hour
And then sleep two.
In your dream you'll eat the mummy cat
And leave the daddy cat to me.
Sleep, my troublemaker.
Mama will sing you a song:
How sweetly
Our chest smells
Of sugar,
And on the floor
There's a crust of bread
In the corner.
The crust wants
To sleep too.
Why are you jumping
Around like that?
Don't be afraid, silly:
That's a cricket
Chirring.
Not a soul in the house –
Dead quiet.
Don't scratch,
Don't make a sound,
Lest the Bogey Man
Should come!
Sleep big ears,
Bye byes.

They brought up their young
Cautiously, as though under the broom.
They told them – be quiet, be quiet –
The cat is vicious and the master too.
The cat will eat you,
The master poison you.
Life's not a song – don't try to be brave!
They'll wipe you out – it's their right,
And no one will say to them 'Shoo!'

The quietest little mouse listened,
And got the drift,
But a chunk of sausage
Brought down his obedient soul.
The mousetrap – that's how it is –
Limits even the humble.
His mama grieved,
His papa turned grey.
The cleverest little mouse thought:
Since the master is the strongest
I'll collaborate with him
And ensure my success.
From a timid creature
I'll turn into man's colleague.
He filled in the form, got to the lab,
But then stopped writing.
The smartest little mouse
Also did not want to obey the elders.
He said: 'What's it come to,
I am not a horse to be led by the bridle;
All my mouse life to live in fear
For a crust or two . . .
Let's get going from here, brothers.
Let's be free spirits
In the open field. Not as slaves or thieves –
We will build such holes
In the old tree by the river,
And such metal trunks.
We'll sow barley and lay on
Water and not count the labour . . .'
He who has tasted freedom
Will never return to the house of the cat.
How he bared his tiny soul,
This little dissident.
Well, all right, old tower,
We'll do without a "happy ending".
A "happy ending" is cat soup,
Is the crowd of mice, rejoicing . . .
Laugh, nanny, with your toothless mouth.
It all happened a long time ago,
I cannot remember what happened next.
Shall I begin another?

The other tale is simple:
Somebody's son in a city somewhere...
But, look, dawn is breaking!
Don't yawn, strike the hour!
Proclaim to all the tormented and the sleepless
That we've made it through the night.
Mountains of snow and silver
Soar beyond the forced peals.

Day Song of the Tower

Oh yes, grief is no disaster.
Time will be,
Time is rubbish.
But I know –
Grey hair –
There is no such
Word: forever,
That hours
Are ice figures –
Spring water
Will sweep them away –
That sadness
Is a furrow in the snow!
The dark star
Is not eternal.
Let the prison transport
Trains go.
Look,
Years change,
A dense queue
Behind,
A high ridge
Ahead!

I write on and the night is over,
And the morning knocks on the bars
With two wings. It's time to crumble the bread
And sprinkle it on the windowsill. It's time to live.
To exercise until I sweat. Then to shiver
From freezing water. So there can be not a trace
Left of sleeplessness.
A crust. A couple of Polish books.
I force myself to crunch through the language,
Half-forgotten, yet so much my own.
Suddenly. Can it be? My head spins.
'You will be a fine lady, a fine lady
At a great court,
And I a black priest, a black priest
In a white monastery.'
That song. I remember twenty lines
And it always makes me cry. A big kerchief.
I am wrapped in it. And my grandma's hands
Tying it crosswise – 'May God protect . . .'
A simple rite,
Incomprehensible, but familiar to me.
Beyond the boundary of memory, in a forgotten childhood
        dream,
That song! What meeting can there be here,
In the branded book, after the word "honour"?
Well no fewer than twenty have passed.
And I am on my predestined road,
And you my prince are beside me. How much easier
It is for the two of us to go into this sweet smoke
Of our kind fatherland! Into the fire!
Into the choking cell. Then into the concrete yard
Five paces wide, and then to the transport
With an Alsatian at our heels –
All in that time, that unknown term.
We'll scorn the not-so-distant "distant".
We are together! Those who are united,
Who have grown together, cannot be parted.
Without you no day, no thought passes. Do you hear
My heart beating through the concrete? But no cry or groan,
A calm calculation. Like the surf on the harbour wall.
This is how we must live. Hearts beating together.

This is how we must go to the trial. To embrace if only in
        our thoughts,
To see each other again, if only for a quarter of a day.
To breathe out the only words,
To kiss the only hand,
Your hand.
To share the same bench –
The first circle, the wings of the first snowstorms.

KGB Prison Kiev, 3 November 1982

[RMcK/HS]

'Over the cornfields'

Over the cornfields roamed the pre-war wind,
And an odd fifth-form boy, in love with everything in the world,
Using whole candles over MAGELLAN's maps,
Was meanwhile growing up. Everything was going
According to plan, wasn't it, Lord? Under the cold sky
He raved about all countries, mixing up fact and fable.
'The orange groves of Sorrento,' he'd whisper, and feel
The strange words spread his soul with sadness.
'The barbarians have descended into the valley,' he'd repeat in Latin,
And, as from captivity, his heart would strain towards that valley.
And when his local town, Izyum, was snowed up,
He'd read of how the slavegirls, tramping the grapes with their feet,
Would dance above the vat to the laughter of copper bracelets,
And this would make his throat go dry as last summer.
From the wall his great-grandfather smiled in his stretch-tight
        buckskins
Eternally young, but having lost a lot of lustre.
The glazed December stood like the clock in the dining room,
Looking and waiting, never saying a word.
And then spring, the sloven, in her wet stockings
Came bustling, laughing, and kissed the hollow
At his temples – and the boy would grow speechless from her gibes.
All the lessons – head over heels! All the rules – mixed up!
He ran to look at the river's ice-drift, and the April wind
Blew the clouds as from a bubble-pipe. MARCUS AURELIUS
Waited with classical patience, open at the same page.
They were selling pickled apples. The birds had frozen
In the blue-eyed abyss, higher than the bells!
And for this sadness there were already not enough words.
And the hands of the fatherland were touching his hair . . .
He had just reached the age to enlist when it began.
He died, as he'd dreamed he would, in battle, defending the flag.
We'd like to know – why we are treated like this, Lord?
We don't know.

Small Zone, 2 May 1983

[DMcD]

'A clumsy saw'

(to Tanya Velikanova)

A clumsy saw,
Plenty of sawdust.
Pre-autumn work.
Let's live till exile!
Soon, soon you'll be joining the convoy,
Soon you'll be putting on a warm sweater,
And freedom will be treading on your heels,
Half with cursing
Half with searches and spying.
We'll saw through the year nineteen eighty-three
– With salt to eat, but without bread –
Right down to the last crunching bits,
Until at last it gives at the seams.
And they won't find out.
Outside the gate, outside the perimeter –
With every note higher,
Our quiet angel will have flown away.
Fate will see to our tasks –
Just let's survive!
Well, until we meet somewhere.
Here's, until we meet somewhere.
Here's Zeks' luck –
Smile!
Bon Voyage.
I've no strength to say farewell.

Small Zone, 1 September 1983

[DMcD]

'So tomorrow, our little ship, Small Zone'

So tomorrow, our little ship, Small Zone,
What will come true for us?
According to what law –
Like an eggshell over dead waves?
Covered in patches and scars,
On the word – the honest word – alone –
By whose hand is our ship preserved,
Our little home?
Those of us who sail to the end, row, live to the end –
Let them tell for the others:
We knew
The touch of this hand.

Small Zone, 18 September 1983

[DMcD]

'I remember an abandoned church'

I remember an abandoned church near Moscow:
The door ajar, and the cupola shattered.
And, screening her child with her hand,
The Virgin Mother quietly mourning –
That the boy's feet are bare,
And once again the cold is at hand
That it's so terrible
To let one's dark-eyed child
Walk off across the snows of Russia – forever – no one
        knows where –
To be crucified by this people, too...
Don't throw stones, it isn't necessary!
Must it really happen again and again –
For love, salvation and miracle,
For his open, undaunted gaze –
That here is to be found a Russian Judas,
That the Russian Pilate is reborn?
But among us, who have come in, there's not a cry,
Not a breath – there's a cramp in our throats:
Across her motherly face
Scratched by broken glass
Are the rough letters of obscene graffiti!
And the infant gazes, as though he were watching an
        execution.
Wait – I will soon come to you!
In your northern December
My face will burn, but I shall tread
The bloodstained Russian road to the end;
But I will ask you – in your power and glory –
What have you done to my Father's house?
And we shall stand before him, sculptedly
Created according to His likeness,
And He will knock on our accursed temples
With the sense of a common guilt.
How much longer – on crosses and on executioner's blocks
Through the fire of a mother's anxiety –
Must we clean from shame and filth
His desecrated image?

How much longer must we wash the earth clean
Of violence and lies?
Do you hear, O Lord? If you hear –
Give us the strength to serve her.

Small Zone, 12 October 1983

[DMcD]

'I will travel through the land'
(to Tanya and Vanya)*

I will travel through the land –
With my retinue of guards,
I will study the eyes of human suffering,
I will see what no one has seen –
But will I be able to describe it?
Will I cry how we are able to do this –
Walk on partings as on water?
How we begin to look like our husbands –
Our eyes, foreheads, the corners of our mouths.
How we remember them – down to each last vein of their skins –
They who have been wrenched away from us for years,
How we write to them: 'Never mind,
You and I are one and the same,
Can't be taken apart!'
And, forged in land,
'Forever' sounds in answer –
That most ancient of words
Behind which, without shadow, is the light.
I will trudge with the convoy,
And I will remember everything –
By heart! – they won't be able to take it from me! –
How we breathe –
Each breath outside the law!
What we live by –
Until the morrow.

Small Zone, 12 November 1983

[DMcD]

* Tatyana Osipova and Ivan Kovalyov.

'I will live and survive'

I will live and survive and be asked:
How they slammed my head against a trestle,
How I had to freeze at nights,
How my hair started to turn grey...
But I'll smile. And will crack some joke
And brush away the encroaching shadow.
And I will render homage to the dry September
That became my second birth.
And I'll be asked: 'Doesn't it hurt you to remember?'
Not being deceived by my outward flippancy.
But the former names will detonate my memory –
Magnificent as old cannon.
And I will tell of the best people in all the earth,
The most tender, but also the most invincible,
How they said farewell, how they went to be tortured,
How they waited for letters from their loved ones.
And I'll be asked: what helped us to live
When there were neither letters nor any news – only walls,
And the cold of the cell, and the blather of official lies,
And the sickening promises made in exchange for betrayal.
And I will tell of the first beauty
I saw in captivity.
A frost-covered window! No spyholes, nor walls,
Nor cell-bars, nor the long-endured pain –
Only a blue radiance on a tiny pane of glass,
A cast pattern – none more beautiful could be dreamt!
The more clearly you looked, the more powerfully blossomed
Those brigand forests, campfires and birds!
And how many times there was bitter cold weather
And how many windows sparkled after that one –
But never was it repeated,
That upheaval of rainbow ice!
And anyway, what good would it be to me now,
And what would be the pretext for that festival?
Such a gift can only be received once,
And perhaps is only needed once.

Labour camp hospital, 30 November 1983

[DMcD]

'I sit on the floor'

I sit on the floor, leaning against the radiator –
A southerner, no-gooder!
Long shadows stretch from the grating, following the lamp.
It's very cold.
You want to roll yourself into a ball, chicken-style.
Silently I listen to the night,
Tucking my chin between my knees.
A quiet rumble along the pipe:
Maybe they'll send hot water in!
But it's doubtful.
The climate's SHIZO. Cainozoic era.
What will warm us quicker – a firm ode of Derzhavin,
A disfavoured greeting of Martial,
Or Homer's bronze?
Mashka Mouse has filched a rusk
And is nibbling it behind the latrine pail.
A two-inch robber,
The most innocent thief in the world.
Outside the window there's a bustle –
And into our cell bursts –
Fresh from freedom –
The December brigand wind.
The pride of the Helsinki group doesn't sleep –
I can hear them by their breathing.
In the Perm camp the regime's
Infringer doesn't sleep either.
Somewhere in Kiev another, obsessed,
Is twiddling the knob of the radio . . .
And Orion ascends,
Passing from roof to roof.
And the sad tale of Russia
(Maybe we are only dreaming?)
Makes room for Mashka Mouse, and us and the radio set,
On the clean page, not yet begun,
Opening this long winter
On tomorrow.

SHIZO, 16 December 1983   [DMcD]

28

'Let's be sad'
(for Ilyusha)

Let's be sad about our teaspoonful of love
My far-off friend! About the fact
Our prison terms are endless,
That all the prophets are so stern –
Ah, if only someone would bless us!
My friend, let's be sad about how
I came running in from March;
You were waiting in the doorway.
And took me into that
Good house. And the curtain of the station
Was so delayed that the hastily
Torn-off sprig had time to flower –
And the narrow cupboard of a room floated
Into a shyness the colour of wax.
Let's be sad that we're
Still so profusely young –
But we, who've been born in an alien land,
With our fate of wandering and pride –
Should we seek to borrow a native land?
Like a bell fallen silent
Is the heart's spasm.
How fathomlessly void is all ahead of us!
But even the very longest sadness
Has a single smile at last.

SHIZO, 30 December 1983

[DMcD]

29

To my unknown friend

Above my half of the world
The comets spread their tails.
In my half of the century
Half the world looks me in the eye.
In my hemisphere the wind's blowing,
There are feasts of plague without end.
But a searchlight shines in our faces,
And effaces the touch of death.
And our madness retreats from us,
And our sadness passes through us,
And we stand in the midst of our fates,
Setting our shoulders against the plague.
We shall hold it back with our selves,
We shall stride through the nightmare.
It will not get further than us – don't be afraid
On the other side of the globe!

Small Zone, 26 February 1984

[DMcD]

'Like Mandelstam's swallow'

Like Mandelstam's swallow
Parting falls towards the heart,
Pasternak sends the rain,
And Tsvetayeva – the wind.
So that the Universe's turning may be achieved
Without a false note,
The word is needed – and poets alone
Are answerable for this.
And the peals of spring whirl by
Over Tyutchevian waters,
And autumn's classical music breaks through
Again and again.
But no one's voice has yet
Winged its way to freedom,
Nor performed freedom, *svoboda*,
Even though it's a Russian word.

Small Zone, 25 April 1984

[DMcD]

'The wind changed'

The wind changed,
And the new wind was autocratic.
The sky was raised like a siege
And took the suburbs.
Behind the northern wall
The horses snorted in peals,
But the first cohorts smashed through
The breach in the eastern gate.
And at once the remains of the towers
Vanished in the smoky gap,
Along with the crosses and bells.
My city resisted,
It was magnificent and terrible.
It melted in the roaring sky,
Entirely drowned by it.
And later, when the thunderclouds
And the waters had closed above us –
No one knew their victory
Or sang the praises of the dawn.
And since then they have had no peace,
They keep moulding, moulding someone –
Helplessly reproducing
Now a hand, now a garment's hem.

SHIZO, 2 July 1984

[DMcD]

'For the cry from the well'

For the cry from the well of 'mama!'
For the crucifix torn from the wall,
For the lie of your 'telegrams'
When there's an order for an arrest –
I will dream of you, Russia.
In the accursedness of your victories,
In the anguish of your impotence,
In the nausea of your hangover –
Why will fear break through?
All has been mourned, all have been sung to rest –
Who will you flinch from all of a sudden?
Though you'll deny it, take refuge in illusion,
Put all the blame on those who have been killed –
I will still come and stand before you
And look into your eyes.

SHIZO, 5 July 1984

[DMcD]

The white-hot blizzard

We are branded with Russia
By a white-hot blizzard,
By the mad labyrinth of dark craters,
Cavities under the snow:
Go away, eyeless woman, go away!
Only how are we to leave each other,
In our infinite whirling,
In our kinship and conflict with her?

And when at last you break loose
From the oppressive tenderness
Of her despotic embraces,
In which to fall asleep is to do so forever:
Your head swims,
As from the first childish drag at a cigarette,
And your lungs are torn to shreds
Like a cheap envelope.

And then, as you wait for everything that
Has emerged alive from her unpeopled cold
To recover from the narcosis –
To know that the angels of Russia
Freeze to death towards morning
Like sparrows in the frost
Falling from their wires into the snow.

PKT, 4 August 1984

[DMcD]

Rooks

It's those rooks that troubled my soul –
Black-winged like a coquettish fan.
It's they with their snowstorms' chaos
Who put me under a spell:
Pain shuddered alive –
That common one that I lullaby at night,
That everyday one that does not demand an executioner,
Beaten up
By the wing into pitch black,
Not of yesterday,
But a hundred times over – pain.
I was never tempted by any other road,
I mustered strength for all farewells:
To withstand, not to falter at the last stroke.
But for these I did not have the strength.
Even your prayers did not protect me:
Across all turbulent shores –
Consumed in the fire
Of delusion, of wind from afar,
Anguish gushes from the veins.
Fly away, I cannot bear to say farewell.
Yours is another sky, with other laws.
Russia will not bury you in snow
And you will not have to freeze your black steel wings here.
Your road is in the clouds –
Lighter than light,
A fine migratory
Good morning!
Fly away – get out of my sight!
How many more times will I see you off?

Potmin Transit Prison, 30 October 1984

[RMcK/HS]

'We have learned'

We have learned, indeed, to throw time into tins
And have stirred in the condensed night at all times.
This century grows ever darker, and the next will not come soon,
To wipe clean the names off yesterday's prison wall.

We loaded it with the voices of departing friends,
With the names of unborn children – for a new wall.
We equipped it so lovingly, but we ourselves
Do not row in it, we are not even allowed on board.

But covering the measured-out load with coarse matting
We still manage to broadcast the seed.
Our hands are torn but we still pluck out the dragon's
Teeth from the crops, which are fated to stand after us.

SHIZO, November 1984

[RMcK/HS]

'Try to cover your shivering shoulders'

Try to cover your shivering shoulders in rags of the oldest,
Though your dress has great holes in, hugging it close to
      your breast
With that useless adjustment, knowing there's no pin to hold it,
All the fever of freedom degrading to evenings of coldness
And how many such evenings to live through can only be
      guessed.
And what is it for?
For the sake of what vision inviting?
Surely not for that country where hands are for hiding
      behind,
Where from tomb-tops they watch whether everyone finds it
      exciting?
But rebellious children keep exercise books for their writing,
Know how to hide them from dads who from birth have
      been blind.
Discard what is past then,
Those booklets and songs need suppressing,
Do not fear to grow wings since you're destined for life after
      all!
But a boat sails the Lethe, a paper boat bearing a blessing
And these words you unpick:
'You must die' – but is that so distressing?
You just feel slightly sick,
As you enter the stain on the wall.

SHIZO, November 1984

[AM]

'But only not to think'

... But only not to think about the journey
On roads hot, dusty, to be walked all day.
Preserve me, my uncompromising reason,
Don't let the reins go now, only half-way.

A long time yet we must fight off together
The suffocating nights, the prison airs,
The prison dreams – hallucinations, almost,
The senseless gibes of executioners,

The treachery of the wearied, and their kisses'
Poison ... Die, but afterwards fight on –
Not knowing how long the term, and not possessing
The right yet to declare our strength is done.

Don't let us weaken; punish with refusal
Each childish 'Can't take any more, I'm through ...'
Preserve me in this midnight age, my reason.
Keep me from harm – and I'll watch over you.

Small Zone, November 1984

[DMcD]

'Isn't it time to return?'

Isn't it time to return?
We've overstayed our welcome.
Our canals will dry out and our winds will die down.
Our horses will grow wild and the planets will stop still.
Isn't it time, O Father
To return home from distant shores?
All that You order we shall leave here:
Our breath, our labour
And our sorrow too.
But through the length and breadth of this earth
You can see for Yourself:
On every path we are identified
By our eyes.
Against every wall we are shot
Without trial.
How often must we die before You say 'yes'?
Isn't it time to return –
We have paid our debts in full –
For ourselves and also for others.
A hundred times betrayed, all is fulfilled – what more?
Which avalanche must we stop with our shoulders?
Into what struggle must we hurl
Ourselves between two enemies?
And which sky must we hold up?
Our horses are waiting, Father,
Our pastures are bare!
Look – we have gone down all the appointed roads,
And have carved here on stone
All the words that need to be said
For the right to go
Without a backward look.

SHIZO, December 1984

[HS/RMcK]

Before battle

Before battle
Stallions crop the clover on tomorrow's field of battle.
The commanders
Take their compasses and measure – which field hardly matters!
Still unwatered
By the rain of lead or blood, the tracks of tiny creatures.
Comes the morning –
Thunder, and the pale horseman reveals his features.
Before battle
Unseasoned soldiers listen to old sweats boasting.
Their officers
Write their letters, and later someone will pluck guitar-strings.
Towards nightfall
The grass is hushed and smells of honey and heavy pollen.
Comes the morning –
Thunder, and any letters will be from the fallen.

SHIZO, December 1984

[AM]

40

'If it's a long snowy walk'

If it's a long snowy walk from the bus,
Steering by the stars rather than the street lamps,
Then frost will melt on your lips like unripe cloudberries
And the house in mid-January will seem to be a ship.

We climb the steps as though rescued on board
And the dark door opens to the icicle key,
And the customary swift shadows of the company which
        make
Mischief in the night emptiness, skitter to the side.

The tap in the kitchen whimpers like a puppy, and the
        floorboard
Squeaks and complains to the owners arriving back late,
And the youngster moon, frozen on its long watch,
Thrusts its horns at the window, like any little beast of the
        Earth.

We shall kindle a fire, so that good people may come,
So that the bell may ring and ring at our gate ...
If the road is long – all this will come to pass –
In mid-January,
But which January?

Small Zone, January 1985

[RMcK/HS]

Lady Godiva

How little I know of you,
Golden-maned lady!
Not the why of your exile,
Nor what happened later...
Just a snippet of a legend
Tells your wordless triumph
Over that high and mighty churl,
Tells how shuttered windows
Served you as shield,
And a disciplined popular will:
No mocking allowed!
(How can one help but love the English?)
A town without people,
All its gates shut tight:
Not a soul unless
You count the executioner.
Did this executioner exist?
Maybe I just invented him?
But in such affairs
Can he be avoided?
As a judge will play the devil,
A gravedigger dig the grave,
So the executioner stands waiting
Beside every deathless road.
But the executioner's eyes
Can't be seen through the slit in his hood,
As it was and always has been –
(Perhaps they're not meant to have eyes?)
In the whole world, just those two:
The Earl of Mercia on his balcony,
The eyeless executioner,
See you off into exile.
The drumming of hooves
Dies away along empty streets
Like a forgotten word
Plunged into rustling centuries.

Here time has jammed in still motion,
And the wind doesn't dare to touch
The inconceivable cloak
Of heavy hair.
Oh, courageous lady,
Let's fearlessly spur the horse,
Ride straight ahead,
Not counting centuries or minutes!
Let's slice executions and epochs
Like pieces of layer cake,
And cut through other epochs
Following close on our heels!
We'll wear a hole in history –
When was it sorry for us?
We'll take a corner off the town's town hall,
Frighten the pettifoggers,
Break into somebody else's years
With our crazy steed
Reflecting the divided world
In one astonished pupil!

Small Zone, January 1985

[LC/SS]

'And when you are cut down'

And when you are cut down in battle,
You'll see numerous people arrive.
Before you are buried they'll scatter
Handfuls of earth on your grave.
Some were friends, some acquaintances, merely.
Just look at the size of the crowd!
So there's nothing peculiar, really,
If the lumps of earth turn into mud.
Some hint at it, others proclaim it:
This dying for freedom, why bother?
You haven't done much for their climate –
So here's mud
From their own rotten weather.

Small Zone, January 1985

[CR]

44

'Our sky'

Our sky has a hard enough dome
Like the chill of laboratory glass.
Our earth lasts a long enough time –
We'll die before either of these.
But still we go on writing letters
In spite of the bare winter days.
Didn't you realise, Creator,
Homuncules have obstinate ways?
And they'll breed other obstinate creatures,
Ashamed of a hanging head,
Well able to meet, gazing upwards,
The descending gaze of God.
Is it such a surprise, oh Creator,
If, in your experiment, that
Humility which was intended
For ordinary mortals, runs out?
Take care when we rush to each other.
Hold on to your chemistry set!
Build a labyrinth for us. We'll uncover
The secret of gunpowder yet!
And to counter the torments of death
We'll invent a triumphant phrase.
And smile at the pain through our teeth
Reminding you of – Whom else?
The law was created by You –
That clay becomes stronger when fired,
And if one and one have to make two
A test-tube can't tell them – divide.
Peer into the flickering glass,
Make a gesture to say we can go.
Don't feel like a failure, because
Out of all the herd, you lost two.
It's time to switch off at the mains,
Father, don't hesitate
What more can you add to our pains
Besides everlasting night?

What order remains to be given?
We stand with lifted gaze,
Two proud people, on whom
The light continues to blaze.

Small Zone, January 1985

[CR]

'Only that which rocks'

Only that which rocks in the rhythm
Of the surf is eternal in this world.
In the sky – the black and the blue,
In the centuries – the dust of centuries.
What changes is immortal . . .
Wait, February, let me think!
But the sparrows laugh on the wing,
And the frost breathes spring.
Let's cast off our skins and change our souls
To spring ones, leaving only tufts
Of wool, not sick dreams
Of past or future –
Let's not take them into the April procession!
But go over the still not dry *terra firma*,
Over the spreading folds of the age,
Catching the unexpected wind
Even against the wind when we have to.
And when the bugle sounds the all-clear,
The sky, the black and blue
Will blaze again into our eye sockets
With an eternally familiar call.

Small Zone, February 1985

[RMcK/HS]

Vocation

Today, for God, Michelangelo
Has turned his hand to cloud sculpture.
Look across the deserted shore.
There is the famous signature.
Over water and over towns,
Over the forest's ragged fur
The clouds are swept, and from the highest
Reaches, a solemn mass resounds.
Today, put on your most formal dress
And bare it to the ancient, cold,
Biblical wind. Look, it's the first,
The rarest day in the whole world!
Just wish, and all will be fulfilled.
You have the tools, you have the right.
Heavy bells chime. You pant and yearn
And feel eternity can't contain
Both you and all your territory.
You are the master of your sky:
Can you direct the planets too?
The hardest gift of all remains
To trust yourself and what you do.
But the kinds of clouds you choose to mould
Expand and fill the universe.
So rise and face the world.
Go straight ahead. Go on.
Well, then?
Can you face immortality
With an equal fearlessness?

Small Zone, March 1985

[CR]

48

'The day died'

The day died like a dog and won't come back,
So let's arrange a splendid funeral feast.
There will be many more days just as black,
I know. The further east
You go, the worse it gets
(That's the usual fate of pioneers!)
But evening's slow-paced gladness will revive
Our worn-out sinews like a healing spring.
The day is done. Our blood slows. We're alive,
Though life is harsh, the age unpitying.
We take another lovely draught, and let
The dusk carry us back to some lost place
Where, with our young audacity, we face
Freedom – and accept the price of it.

Small Zone, March 1985

[CR]

'In the evening'

In the evening, a man with a carpet roll
Is walking, who knows where.
And no one will take any notice at all
When he vanishes round the corner –
Nor know what that carpet looked like inside,
Of feathered or furry creation,
And whence he turned up in our yard,
With its mothers in windows, and kids playing hard,
And the silvery heads of old women that nod,
Guarding the memories of three generations,
In our yard, where they know everyone by his name,
Who's alive, who's dead, who's gone off,
And from whose window, who's calling whom,
Piecha's voice sounds rough!*
Past the rattle of dice on the worn table-top,
Past the lecturer's car he goes,
With that carpet roll on his shoulder he plods –
A whiff of dust catches your nose.
Perhaps, this carpet is where the man lives,
And finding a suitable spot,
With the proper incantation he will
Masterfully order it: Spread!
And it will oblige, with all that it's got,
With bookcase and harpsichord,
With a broken-down chair
And a lamp with a flame,
And a son playing with bricks, on board.
And perhaps it's been taught how to fly –
And so, his walk done, his carpet will leap
Straight out of the narrow, deserted street,
And vanish into the sky,
And blissfully smooth itself out, that flexible square
The South Wind will briefly know.
And till dawn the master will smoke his pipe there,
And watch the sparkling town below.

Piecha: someone is playing a record
by Polish singer Edyta Piecha.

And then in the blue he'll dwindle away,
An oddball, a freak,
On his mat,
With an indistinct word he'll drop into the air ...
What can you expect from a fellow like that!

Small Zone, March 1985

[DW]

'Crafty old man'

Crafty old man, in this you weren't a liar.
We are forbidden by eternal doubt
To stop the precious moment in its flight:
And still the mountain-pass may lead us higher.
Perhaps we haven't nearly reached the summit,
Although the smoky fumes of victory
Enchant us, and we follow faithfully,
Blessed, as the young are, by no sense of limit.
But somehow while the precious moment lasts
Our actual height's impossible to judge:
Napoleon looked less fine at Austerlitz
Than when, in youth, he stood on Arkol Bridge.
So who is capable of freezing time
As if it were a bird, shot from the blue?
Happily, we ourselves still dare to climb;
Sedition and ambition see us through.
We have outpaced the future, step for step:
Our deeds have proved us guilty in advance.
If time should raise its hand to us, cry 'Stop!'
We'll just push on, and trample down the fence.

Small Zone, April 1985

[CR]

'Sit down'

Sit down, light up. Such a short time, but we are by
       ourselves.
We won't get anything done: this dream does not have an
       ending.
No time for finding
Out what books are on the shelves,
What roof is over our heads, and what horses are at the
       steps.
They are waiting for us. It's time, and there is no time left
To talk about the years we spent apart.
Our short time together lasts one cigarette,
A silent moment,
Eyes meet eyes and pierce to the heart.
I know that we will carry there where they wait for us
Something more important than us and our losses.
All right, we're ready for the journey,
But let's finish our cigarettes while they saddle the horses,
And clasp hands for grim death, as they unlock the door.

SHIZO, May 1985

[RMcK/HS]

53

A Little Song

If I were a gypsy,
You – a country gent –
I'd sing to you
Parting and greeting.
If I were a dew-drop,
You – a tallish weed –
I'd fall upon you
Every evening.
If I were a river,
You – a bitter ocean –
I'd wash out bitterness
With every motion.
If our families started
A royal feud,
I'd run away, dearest,
Barefoot, to you.
If I had in this world
A little more time,
You'd break through to me,
You'd find a way.
As for one last meeting,
Request it of God.
They tell me he's friendly,
He can help, they say.

SHIZO, May 1985

[LC/SS]

'It's not that I'm scared'

It's not that I'm scared,
Just a little uneasy.
It hurts that I might not bear a son,
As the heart is giving out, and the hands grow weaker –
I try to hold on,
But they just grow weaker, damn them!
I could have written children's books,
And I liked horses,
And also I liked to perch on a favourite cliff,
And jumping into the sea I could pace myself well;
And when I thought I could not get back
I'd still somehow swim to shore.
And I flew in my dreams and shuddered
When I thought my time would come soon.
But the voice had spoken: 'If not I, then who?'
It had spoken so long ago –
I had no choice in the matter.
For they are shameful the endless debates over tea,
For they have perished – the brightest and the best!
Father Alexander, pray for those on the sea –
And for the land
They have left behind.

SHIZO, June 1985

[RMcK/HS]

Jacob

The first soldier of solitude
With no general and no squad,
Endowed with the highest valour –
To fight his terrible God!
With no support, no protection,
Nor behind his back – His breath.
First trial of equals in dispute,
An ordeal as cruel as death.
But he stood – like Him to the pupils,
Never trembling – His handiwork!
Not subservient to fear or hatred –
Until dawn, and death's sweaty murk,
In close combat with the Immortal –
Strong in muscle, the heart of a man!
Not his slave, and not his bondsman –
Giving back the strength he had won
From his God, devoted without fawning,
Without pleading or cowering down.
The proudest of all his victories.
Diadem in his Father's crown.
The first one called who answered,
The first one marked with this hand!
Approaching his insolent grandsons
In glory when sleep won't descend –
Wall of muscles, a stubborn forehead,
A torn tendon's honour and fame!
That in strife they don't call for their mothers,
That they view weakness as shame.
That they seek not the herd but their pathway
That it's freedom they bear in their blood!
But they don't need to strain an artery.
God already knows their brood.

PKT, August 1985

[DMcD]

'Somewhere a pendulum moves'

Somewhere a pendulum moves, and softly a cuckoo is
      weeping,
Why should she count the hours, and not the long years for us.
And in the abandoned house, the old woman opens the
      shutters,
At the appropriate time, and with the same care as before.

Somewhere in the gloom a lamp is burning, the knitting
      continues,
And the rare letters are kept, and news is awaited.
And she, as is her custom, grieves only with her eyes,
And needlessly straightens the portraits of the children who
      have grown.

And what is all this for,
And who before her is not sinful?
And over whom, departing, did she not make the sign of the
      cross?
But the one that she loves, may be comforted, saved.
And the one whom she awaits, may he find her on his
      return.

PKT, September 1985

[DW]

'Stubborn like Sisyphus'

Stubborn
Like Sisyphus
Who rejects the taunts of Zeus
And wrenches out the stone;
Like the Levite
Who dares to unveil the Ark
And touches it with bare hands;
Like a jackdaw
Who breaks a window in flight
From a strange house.
I am stubborn.
If not I, then who?
And again and again:
No, the cold
Will not reach beyond consciousness –
Warm rivers flow there! –
Nor time –
The fool who fights us
Over the words 'for ever',
But even parting
Is in shoddy disguise, even captivity
Is in clown's insignia.
Lifelong torment
For immortal souls – a threat? – a joke!
So let us all laugh together.

PKT, September 1985

[HS/RMcK]

'When you comb your hair'

When you comb your hair, the forgotten lock
Means a journey.
So let us go – God be with us – nothing to lose
From dungeon to dungeon.

Through the chink in the iron the same refrain
Of birches and fences.
Write to us and forgive us our delay:
You'll get no speedy answers.

Stones hit the floor, this shaking means
The van's bumping over railway sleepers.
No time to sightsee – aching bones,
That chink in the iron disappears.

Which dusty road are we measuring?
Which centuries?
On our bodies we shall go on treasuring
The hard Earth's unevenness

But some day, some year, we'll get out.
Maybe we will return.
Send us your letters, whether they reach us or not,
One day we'll read every one.

PKT, September 1985

[HS/RMcK]

'Tomorrow or today'

Tomorrow or today
They promised showers,
Promised coloured peas
With the hail.
I'll take my bag
And you take one too,
And perhaps there'll be
Some cakes after all.
These forecasts, you know,
Are questionable.
Weathermen are only human,
They can get it wrong.
The climate is such nowadays,
Storms and cyclones,
Even radio waves
Cannot get through.
In England it rains
Cats and dogs,
Whereas in Bermuda
It rains frogs,
But with us it's rags,
Torn galoshes,
A superfluous alphabet.
And dead souls.
Such precipitations
By their disarray,
Do, of course, get in the way –
They're such a nuisance.
Torn galoshes
Ruin the harvest
And there's graffiti
On every fence.
But this is a temporary situation,
Tomorrow will be better.
They've promised us
Coloured peas!

When heaps and heaps
Fall from the sky
You and I will get
A sprinkling too.
Perhaps this sort of shower
Has already fallen somewhere.
It's been reported
They've been dished out in Kaluga.
So don't worry,
It'll come to us too.
Sir, is this the end of the queue?
I'll stand behind you.

PKT, 9 October 1985

[RMcK/HS]

'The damp here'

The damp here makes voices hoarse
But they can still break through the slime of cement.
Not for nothing do clouds, like a regiment of horse,
Crowd together above the Mordovian land.
They have felt it all – on their own skin,
And despite the sticky mire,
They can be thoughtful, bright or grim
But always incredibly high.
Here they have all seen so much pain
That they will bear without flinching the convict's stare.
Sometimes breaking down they cry buckets over the field . . .
Taste the bread – it is a little bitter.
There's no tampering with these stubborn witnesses,
No reaching them, no stuffing them into prisons.
The snow will fall thickly like evidence
Onto your roofs, umbrellas, mackintoshes.
The unsolicited truth stares you in the face,
It does not spare the clever or the stupid . . .
With white conscience they'll cover the city streets
To make you shudder before you step on them.
The next in line come flocking,
Born of whose breath,
Of which woman's moans?
Silently they float abo᾿e Mordovia again –
We can see them throᴜgh the stones.

PKT, October 1985

[HS/RMcK]

'And if sleep doesn't come'

And if sleep doesn't come, count up to a hundred,
And chase away these thoughts.
I know, you can't reach me any longer,
And nothing can help any more.
So when at night you're burning, don't rend
The white bandage of your last sleep!
Perhaps I shall come again soon, and then
Surely you'll recognise me.
And I shall be like a child, like a bush –
With the tenderest touch of all.
And you, predict something longer for me,
A tale with a happy end.
And I shall be like grass, or like sand –
So I'm warmer to embrace.
But if I'm like a starving hound –
Feed me without delay.
Like a gypsy, I shall snatch at your sleeve,
Hurl myself, like a bird, at your pane.
Don't chase me away, when you know who I am.
All I want to do is look in.
And one of these days, in foreign parts,
In the snow, or maybe the rain,
Upon a frozen kitten you'll chance,
And it will be me again.
And whomever you please, whatever his plight,
You'll be able to save, come what may.
And I at that time will be everywhere,
Everywhere on your way.

PKT, October 1985

[DW]

'The dawn chill'

The dawn chill at the year's declension –
My heart, now falling in with this,
A state permitting no dissension,
Grows numb, aware of the abyss.

Your tousled mop when rising seven
Still holds the pleasant warmth of milk;
Cold things seek vengeance on the living –
The tiles, the window-panes, oiled silk.

And mother, cold lips pursed and certain:
– Now make your bed! Your books for class!
... And brush my hair. And wash my glass.
The icy light beyond the curtain

Is not so alien, it would seem,
As this unyielding stone regime!
How many years?
Whose will is stronger?

The jingling guard-chain falls; a click.
Now slam the door.
And get out quick.

PKT, October 1985

[AM]

64

'We have learned to say goodbye'
(for Valery Senderov)

We have learnt to say goodbye.
They are taken away from us, they go away,
And at times someone sees us off, too.
And the rails like two knives
Slice the white distance . . .
Our lives begin in wandering,
We cannot be restrained.
So hard to look around.
And the wheels – faster, faster . . .
We know it is easier for those who leave.
Those who stay shuffle home,
Carrying the station's emptiness.
They amble round the room in silence.
No point in putting on the light
Or making cups of tea.
We have learnt to release
Our friends' responsive hands.
But in some far off circle
The familiar yearning
Reaches us steadily.
It seeks out our hearts
By name
For life.
We are its drafts,
The palettes of an insane brush,
The targets of ruthless truths –
We are all its pupils,
And we know its secrets:
The cigarettes at night
And ringing telephones.
But I do not remember swearing
It allegiance.
Marked by the convict's brand
Of its sleepless labour,
Without counting our losses,
Desperately we disbelieve it.
And in our daring years
We thoughtlessly whistle

Its cruel tunes,
Just because we are alive
And there is someone who can
Contradict it stubbornly
And say that journeys end
In meetings of the parted.

SHIZO, November 1985

[HS/RMcK]

To the Children of Prison Warden Akimkina

In this year – the year seven thousand,
Five hundred and ninety four
Since the beginning of time –
It snowed continuously.
Each morning the sky's blade hardened
With a particular glare.
The sky and the earth's white rim
Were a single entity.
Russia was where it happened –
Mordovia, to be exact –
The nation which joined with Russia
Five hundred years ago.
For this most distinguished act
She received an Order of Merit
Which is still being talked about
And discussed on the radio.
And they sing about lyrical groves –
Birch-groves, naturally.
On the transport, it's hard to see
So you learn to believe your ears.
In this place, fences are grown;
Watch-towers stick up like splinters,
And, under the wind, the bales
Of wire sound like dried-up reeds.
Wild animals also roam –
Snarling dogs, trained for service.
Without them, there'd be no camp,
No transport, no prison sentence.
They're the tried and tested guards
For all nations and all occasions;
No one can argue with them.
The bread they gobble, they earn.
And the sky above this land
Has become a permanent fixture.
You can't will it to move away,
Though you stare at it for years.
If it's frozen utterly
This is the law of nature
Carried out as predetermined
Whenever December occurs.

It had snowed for four whole days.
The girls froze in their cell.
They weren't very old; the eldest
Was twenty-one, no more.
'Madam,' they said 'At least
Pour us some boiling water!
And couldn't you give us some tights
If we've got to sit on the floor?'
'You bitches,' came the reply:
'So what else would you like?
You'd get nothing if I had my way,
You scroungers, not one bite.
D'you want some bedclothes, some boots?
If I had my way, you pigs,
You'd be in your birthday suits.'
Of course, they deserved this lot.
They were lucky not to get worse.
The bosses don't make mistakes
And put you inside without cause.
It's winter, so let them freeze.
Why should their stoves be hot?
That's what SHIZO's all about:
They won't be back in a hurry.
It's not as if they're naked:
They've got their prison-smocks.
And they haven't much time to do
Anyway, so why worry?
They're already worn out. They lie
On the floor, in spite of the cold,
While the prison mice fearlessly
Scamper across their faces.
Nobody's died. They'll be freed
After a spell in SHIZO.
Don't waste your sympathy.
They're invalids, not war-heroes.
Some will get out in ten days,
Some in a fortnight or less.
And if a short spell below zero's
Injured their health, who cares?
It's part of the punishment.
Let them serve their time, and then
They can go somewhere for treatment.

We've got problems of our own.
The fact that they can't have children
Is something they still don't know.
If you think clearly about it,
It's none of their business to know.
Of course, it will all come out later.
They'll go from doctor to doctor,
Frantic with hope, as they try
To work out their dates, but mistaken.
They'll cry in the corridors
Of countless maternity clinics.
Through endless appointments they'll cry,
And at night a thin voice will wake them:
'Are you listening, Mummy?
Listen, listen to me.
Do you remember you dreamt
That you'd given birth to me?
Now the mice, the grey mice
Have eaten me up.
Where are you,
Where are you,
Where were you then?
Mummy, mummy, I'm cold.
Put me a nappy on.
I'm frightened of being alone.
Why don't you come to me?
You wanted a baby girl
Remember?
Remember?
Why don't you come
Why don't you?
Aren't you even waiting for me?'
But what, in fact, really happened?
Plenty of others are crying
In the maternity home.
We have no shortage of people.
There are millions and millions of them.
We can find people to build
Factories, furnaces, shops;
People who'll do what they're told
And people who'll get to the top.
It isn't so bad, after all,

On the broad, historical scale.
And no, we won't sacrifice
Our work and our songs and our dreams
Today, in the year seven thousand,
Five hundred and ninety-four –
A figure too shameful to count,
If you start from the birth of Christ.

PKT, December 1985

[CR]

Chipmunk

Weeping and lamenting,
The chipmunk sits:
'Now where am I going to
Find any nuts!
Haven't I been searching
For days on end?
And didn't I hide them
Under the ground?
Didn't I pack them
Into my cheeks,
Each, my chosen one,
Chosen by me, each!
All kinds of nasty customers
Are on the loose.
Now one's found my storehouse.
Shouldn't he be asking: Whose?
No, he doesn't bother,
Slides his paws right in,
And the nuts are rolling round,
And all he does is grin!
Look, he's stopped, he's smirking,
That old bear's snout!
May you break a tooth
On the hardest one, you lout!'
But a crow makes fun:
'Listen, flabface, lay
A larger stock in next time,
Don't give the game away!'
'Oh I'm so unlucky,
From number one to five,
Stripes along my back,
Mi-se-ra-ble stripes!
My paws aren't worth a penny,
My tail is an excuse!
That ruffian has robbed me,
He's cleaned me out, the brute!
He should have his ears boxed,
Get what he deserves!
Mama, why'd you bring me

Like this into the world,
Such a puny fellow,
Such a nobody.
Listen, Mama chipmunk,
Give birth again to me:
So bitter sorrow shouldn't
Be my lot in life here;
If stripes are what I'm stuck with,
So let me be a tiger!'

PKT, 30 December 1985

[DW]

'The stars have flown'

The stars have flown, but we still dare wish.
A snowflake falls, no worse in size than a star.
Foretell us a miracle with a solemn childish faith,
Not in vain did the guest's bold hand burn you.

Then another rebelled and broke from the flock
And settled like a bird awkwardly on my shoulder.
It waits for the ineffable word, is slow to melt,
And I whisper hastily, stumblingly –
You know just what.

Over us December bursts its banks.
It is brave as a Hussar, its generosity is without reproach.
But the winter is short,
But we are so eternally young
That the snows of all Russias are not enough for our wishes.

PKT, January 1986

[RMcK/HS]

Song of Long Ago

Forgive me, little sister,
And my little brother,
For not revealing myself,
For not taking you with me.
Beyond the Charred Forest,
I'll gather cranberries,
Alone and lonely,
With a quiet heart.
I'll gather cranberries,
Counting those berries,
I'll forget my sorrow –
As if it had never been.
Beyond the Charred Forest,
A place unbeknown to anyone:
If I sing, if I weep –
Not a soul will answer.
The first berry –
Blood-drop from a bird:
For a pair of swans –
Preordained parting.
There follows the second –
A girl's crimson blood:
Riding Tartars
Let loose their arrows.
But the third berry –
I'll not go near it,
So I won't dream of it at night:
Tomorrow, my intended
Begins his journey,
To return or not –
If God's will be done.

PKT, January 1986

[LC/SS]

'The echoing expanses of high ceilings'

The echoing expanses of high ceilings,
For long already have not been seen by me!
Conservatorium, refuge of windy strings,
Where a mystery hides behind the wall,
Where thoughts are arched,
Voices are unfamiliar,
Where solemn vaults solicitously
Take us, like children, by the chin
And make us raise our eyes!
I'll come to you with a weary heart,
With burns, invisible to the eye,
As into a dark-blue forest of half-remembered tales,
Where everything has always ended well.

PKT, January 1986

[DW]

Song of the Wave

He has left you behind and has come to me –
So how then am I to blame?
Yes, stand all you like at Whitestone Lee –
The ending is still the same.
Don't torture your eyes with the salt sea-spray,
Don't walk by the water's hem.
For of course as I'm breaking, your tracks I'll erase
Like all traces left there by men.
For the fact is my road – for thousands of years –
Was laid down by Him who commands:
So I must keep returning to this piece of earth
Then again fall away from land.
For the stars – one law, and for fish – one law,
And the men of your island race
From birth are fishermen, working the trawl
Till the last great breaker they face.
He has left you behind and has come to me –
He is stubborn, that you must own.
And if my caress is salt as the sea –
It was chosen by him alone.
I'll cast up his pipe by Whitestone Lee,
And amber I'll take from the shore,
For now he is dwelling in far other seas
So ask not to see him more.
I myself will work to fashion his couch –
Silken cushions of sea-grass make,
And then my kisses I'll press on his mouth,
But I'll never call him to wake.
You never will see him, but till you are grey,
Till the final pain in your breast
Like the girls of your land you will take your way
To the shore in your hopeless quest.
You yourself are so stubborn, the same as he,
And I know in the course of time
You will follow his road to other seas,
And I will go on with mine.

And your race the way their fathers took –
Still oceanwards, as before.
And someone will pick up a pipe as he looks
For amber along the shore.

Small Zone, June 1986

[AM]

'Fire for words'

Fire for words and strength for wine,
And lightness and daring glory for the violin bow!
The ancestors smile at us mischievously,
From the dark frames absolve us of guilt
For bringing to life the forgotten epoch
For just one evening, for just one hour.
If we should cause a commotion –
Well, did they have to wake up in us?

KGB Prison, Kiev, August 1986

[RMcK/HS]

78

Rendezvous

Just the same, you and I never know at all
What, today or tomorrow, fate will try.
Our task – to be fearless if misfortunes fall,
And calm, if we need to say goodbye.
Look at me – What an effort smiling takes –
Remember this moment, whatever the cost!
It's not time yet to release the brakes –
The first of the circles has still to be crossed.
I won't cry on a shoulder which torment made hard.
It's not time yet for womanish demonstration.
Five minutes, they'll take me, the way will be barred
By the gate of our new separation.
Start clashing, keys: our souls won't be crushed
By a return ticket's stamp or two.
The time will come – for five minutes, bitter, hushed,
How much credit, in centuries, will we be due?

KGB Prison, Kiev, 13 August 1986

[LC/SS]

'Motherland, you're growing'

Motherland, you're growing into my ribcage.
Wait, slow down, not now!
I remember only fleeting moments of your kindness.
You are savage as an Apocalyptic beast.
Rain yet again thrashes the concrete,
Lashes over the reinforced bars.
Let me take deep breaths of the wind
Through the muzzled window.
I know it's absurd to expect this caress,
So I keep quiet and don't show the pain.
Today I'll take my bread ration,
And put aside the crust for tomorrow.
How many years, bending over my poems
Will I have to hide them, hearing the clank of keys?
Motherland, how many breaths will you dole out to me?
How many cruel cell nights?
Your massive paws squeeze a groan out of me,
It's so difficult to be alive.
Come the day of the last transit stage,
You can push the grasses
Through me and close in silence over me,
And lead off the wind beyond the clouds.
Wait, don't sound the all-clear
I've yet to write the most
Important line.

KGB Prison, Kiev, September 1986

[HS/RMcK]

'The heron walks in the marsh'

The heron walks in the marsh,
Its legs like a pair of compasses.
The cold, like a greenish shadow,
Lies upon the forest.
The air, dense and grey,
Itself lies down under its wing.
Above is the twilit sky,
Below, a network of plants.
Who is playing there with the wind?
Who, altering his voice,
Has called from the forest,
But has not ventured forth?
A ray of forgotten light
Gingerly tests the water.
Now our endless evening
Has gone off on its circular course.
Beasts, people and birds,
And voices, and specks of light –
We pass through all like ripples,
And each one disappears.
Which of us will recur?
Who will flow into whom?
What do we need in this world
To quench our thirst?

Kiev, 9 October 1986

[DW]

'Believe me'

Believe me, it was often thus:
In solitary cells, on winter nights
A sudden sense of joy and warmth
And a resounding note of love.
And then, unsleeping, I would know
A-huddle by an icy wall:
Someone is thinking of me now,
Petitioning the Lord for me.
My dear ones, thank you all
Who did not falter, who believed in us!
In the most fearful prison hour
We probably would not have passed
Through everything – from end to end,
Our heads held high, unbowed –
Without your valiant hearts
To light our path.

Kiev, 10 October 1986

[AK]

'A land of pensive railway stations'

A land of pensive railway stations
And ever-sympathetic wives!
Both weak and strong, your children's lives
You've plagued with doubt and hesitations!
Your endless questions through the darkness
And your reproaches – till I'm grey,
I cannot find convincing answers,
What can I say? What can I say?
With you like this, can we continue?
Against the world you shield your face
And hold your precious self within you:
Forget you? Curse you? Should I bless?

Moscow, 21 October 1986

[AM]

'Somewhere far'
(for Dick Rodgers)

Somewhere far, far away
Is a land I have known since childhood
From books, from fraying maps.
White cliffs rise from the sea as from faraway dreams.
How I dread to awake
And find myself back in the camps!
Somewhere there they awaited me, even as I thought I'd die,
There my friend shared my pain and privations
In an iron-barred cage.
There, deprived of all news
They were deaf to all lies
And not counting the years, tried to save me from dying.
I would write – but the mails go astray,
And the phone has been dead since yesterday morning.
I would fly – but invisible bonds hold my shoulders!
Do not break up that cage, my dear friend,
For it's not yet time.
Let it be, though,
The last in creation!

Kiev, 30 October 1986

[AK]

Lagle Parek

You were blonde, not at all like the natives;
Judicious, clear-eyed, all-discerning.
You brought us Estonian plosives:
'Terre Homikust' to our 'Good Morning!'

The camp-years drag by, every wishful
Letter sighs 'home'. Lagle finds
The weather forecast, read in Russian,
And catches the Baltic winds.

It's six and the sleeping-planks rattle.
Inquisitive fingers of light
Poke the bars. Terre Homikust, Lagle!
We're thinking of you. Don't forget!

Kiev, November 1986

[CR]

'Time falls in creases'

Time falls in creases
And flows down the shoulder.
Listen how the crowd rejoices
Waiting for the executioner.

Drunken people, well-fed horses,
Loud laughter, merry-making;
On each icon, in each house
The Saviour's visage – merciless.

Who is that whirling in the dusk?
Not so fast – it is still light.
Time falls into nooses,
Around our throats – drawing tight.

Kiev, 16 November 1986

[HS/RMcK]

Exodus

Everything repeats itself in life, everything repeats itself:
Again the night road, and the hand holding mine.
Everything changes in the world, everything changes:
If you live a while longer, you'll see that the clock has
       stopped.

And the intricate black fingers are still.
And the sum of scars and insults fades from the heart.
And the stepmother stands silent by your cross.
And you enter the final tunnel, knowing who it is that waits.

In the meantime – the night road and the ticking up of
       numbers.
And the road, unmeasured by us, gathers in the miles.
And my virgin, midnight star stands high and says:
When you say goodbye, take care you don't forget me.

Kiev, 8 December 1986

[BM]

87

'Too soon to say goodbye'

Too soon to say goodbye,
Too soon to say forgive me,
Too soon to send us your instructions:
You know what our luck is like.
Not a door but it will be locked!
Not a net but it will be cast!
Others took to the bottle.
And others just vanished.
Only a few of us left now,
So they're firing at us point blank.
What now? We can read Dostoyevsky;
Chip in roubles – for vodka,
Only a few of us left anyhow.
And we know we must fight to the death.
And we know that cruel blacksmith
Forged us out of some unknown metal,
Perhaps doubting our endurance,
Perhaps expecting us to recant.
No! Give us your instructions!
We swear to fulfil them precisely.
Too soon to despair yet.
You ought to know our luck.

Kiev, 9 December 1986

[HS/RMcK]

'On the walls'

On the walls King Priam is pacing,
Down below the siege-battle flaring.
Like a soul from the flesh escaping –
No vexation and no despairing –
Out of deep ineffable pity
Watching Troy live its final hour,
Bound by oath to the stricken city,
He will never move from this tower.
For a lofty mouthful of parting
He has begged for his son to bury.
All's accomplished at last. No more starting.
There are no more burdens to carry.
Gods and people mark and attend him:
On his face no terror nor anguish.
See him stand there, white-haired, unbending –
As if freeing a slave from bondage.
One last look at the roof-tops smoking,
And the shrine white and helpless, clinging.
Then for him the blood-spurt and choking
From the arrow now loosed and singing.

Kiev, 9 December 1986

[AM]

ORIGINALS

Это всё грязи спутали мне душу —
Черноокрылые, как трубный звар
Это всё три — сумасшедших значена
Замолчали: дрогнула боль живее —
Та, обычная, что залегла не натат,
так пришлась, что не продует пешая
Ошарашенная
крылом — в смоль,
на вчерашняя,
А стократ — боль!
Никогда не льстилась чужой дорогой,
На все провода собирала силы,
Устала, на последнем взмахе не дрогнуть!
А на этих всё-таки не хватило.
И молитвы твоя не уберегла:
через все смещённые берега —
Наваждением, ветром издалека
Обожжённая — хлещет из мил тоска!
Улетайте, прощаться невыносимо!
Вам — иное небо с другим законом.
Не на вас обрушит снега Россия,
И не вам в них стынуть крылом калёным.
Путь вам облаком —
легче лёгкого!
Утра доброго —
Перелётного!
Улетайте — долой с глаз!
Провожаю — в какой раз?   1984

В день избранья Президента
Были мы без документов,
Человеческой одежки,
Утешительной кормёжки,
книжки, кошки,
Вилки-ложки,
Но зато нам дул в окошко
Утешительный озон,
как полоска в ШИЗО.
И пока голосовали,
пировали,
тропи-бали,
Мы сидели и гадали:
Сколько нам добавки дали,
ПКТ или ШИЗО,
И какой тому резон,
Тут режимник прибежал,
Гнусно врал и угрожал,
но по нашим по расчётам
В это время штат Дакота,

И Миссури, и Канзас
Очень радовали нас.
И к отбою, всерьёзно,
Было всё уже понятно.
Полетели мы к батарее,
Хоть она совсем не греет,
С полундурою по рёбрам,
Мы вздохнули...
Ночи доброй —

Господину Президенту,
Вашингтону,
Кеннингтону,
на котором он стоит,
Всем, кто там ещё не спит —
или — бессонный гнусной кажи —
бия зубами дробь не зря,
Завтра — праздник Октября!
Знайте: мы не спим здесь тоже!

6 ноября 1984, ШИЗО

Научились, наверно, закатывать время в консервы,
И сгущённую ночь подмешали во все времена.
Этот век всё темней,
И не скоро придёт двадцать первый,
Чтоб стереть со вчерашней тюремной стены
имена.
Мы его нагрузили
Ушедших друзей голосами,
Нерождённых детей именами — для новой
стени,
Мы с такою любовью его скоряжали, но сами
Ми ему не гребли,
Даже на борт его не звали.
Но отмеренный груз укрывая рогожею грубой,
Мы ещё успеваем горстями просеять зерно,
Чтоб изранить ладони,
Но выбрать драконовы зубы
Из посева, которому взойти после нас суждено.
1984, ШИЗО

Снова кутать бессмысленной рванью озябшие
плечи,
Просвоённое дырами платье свода на груди
Бесполезным движением, уход-закаляешь
несём,
Всей горячей свободой влипрая в сегодняшний
вечер,
И не ведая, скольких таких вечеров впереди,
И во имя чего,
и какого презрения ради?
Неужели для края, где платут в ладони лицо?
Все гробницы следят за всеобщим участьем в па-
раде,
Но мятежные дети ведут голубые тетради,
И умеют их прятать от слепорождённых отцов.
Возрастай из наследства,
Из книжек и песен вчерашних,
Не робей опереться, назначенный к жизни птенец!
Но в летейской воде окрещённый корабли-
дурак-
ный
Разверни и прочти:
— Умирать — это тоже не страшно,   1984,
Лишь немного точней,
Когда входишь в пламя на стене.   ШИЗО

...Но только б не думать о дороге —
Простой линялой — чтоб идти, идти...
Храни меня, храни, рассудок строгий,
Не отпуская узды на полпути!
Ещё нам долго вместе отбиваться
От каторжных удушливых ночей,
Острожных снов — почти галлюцинаций,
Бессмысленных издёвок палачей,
Предательства уставших, и отрядок
Их поцелуев... Судьями, не стесняясь
Не зная срока, не имея права
Сказать, того ведь, что больше нету сил!
Не позволяй сдаться, казни отходом
Ребяческих... больше не могу.
В кромешный ад — храни меня, мой разум,
Храни — и я тебя уберегу.   1984

— 1 —

Ну не то чтоб страшно,
А всё же не по себе.
И обидно, вдруг сына родить уже не успею.
Потому что сердце сдаёт, и руки слабеют:
Я дергаюсь,
но они, проклятые, всё слабей.
Я могла бы детские книжки писать,
и я лошадей любила.
И любила сидеть на загривке своей скалы,
И умела, в море входя, рассчитывать силы,
А когда рассчитывать не на что —
Всё же как-то доплыть.
Я ещё летала во сне, и мороз по коже
Проходила от мысли, что скоро и мне пора.
Но уже прозвучало: „Если не я, то кто же!"
Так давно прозвучало —
мне было бы выбирать.
Потому что стыдно весь век
За чаями спорить,
Потому что поцелуи лучшие всей земли...
Помолитесь, отец Александр,
За ушедших в море.
И ещё — за землю, с которой они ушли.
1985

Леди Годива.

Как мне мало известно про вас,
Ознегривая леди!
Ни причины изгнанья,
Ни что с вами было потом...
Лишь обрывок легенды
О вашей безмолвной победе
Над властительным хамом,
О том, как вам были щитом
Затворенные ставни
И строгая воля народа,
Не позволят глумленья!
(Ну как не любить англичан!)
Обезлюдевший город,
Закрытые глухо ворота —
Ни единой души,
Разве только считать палаша.
Впрочем, был ли палач?
Может быть, я его спинила!
Но в подобных делах
Как же можно его обойти?
Как лукавит судья,
Как могильщик копает могилу —
Так палач ожидает ~~не~~
На каждом бессмертном пути.
Но глаза палача не видны
Сквозь разрез капюшона,
Как во все времена
(может, им не положено глаз?)
В целом мире лишь двое:
Граф Ковентри, глядя с балкона,
Да безглазый палач
Провожают в изгнание вас.
Только топот коня
В переулках пустынных немеет,
Как забытое слово,
Что в шорох веков сорвалось.
Здесь заклинило время стоп-кадром
И ветер не смеет
Шевельнуть небывалым плащом
Из тяжёлых волос.

А не пора ли обратно,
Мы так задержались тут.
Пересохнут наши каналы,
И ветви книг уснут.
Наши кони забудут руку,
А планеты забудут бег.
Не пора ли, Отец,
От чужих берегов — к себе?
Всё, что Ты велишь, мы оставим в этом краю!
И своё дыхание, и труд,
И печаль свою.
Но, пройдя из конца в конец эту землю —
Ты видишь сам —
Мы на каждой тропе опознаны —
По глазам!
Мы у каждой стены расстреляны —
Без суда!
Сколько раз умирать,
пока Ты не скажешь „да"?
Не пора ли обратно,
За себя,
А потом ещё за других.
Мы стократно преданы, всё исполнено — что ещё!
Под какую лавину ещё
Подставлять плечо?
Между двух врагов кидаться —
В какой борьбе?
И какое небо ещё держать на себе?
Наши кони ждут, Отец,
Наши травы медлят расти.
Посмотри —
Мы прошли назначенные пути,
В здешний камень вбрезали
Все слова, что стоит сказать —
Ради права уйти,
не оглядываясь назад.

1985

(margin, vertical)

Которые следом придут.
Продуманной истории
Сегодняшний... палец?
Сквозь паутину..., сквозь
труд судейских крючков,
И в чудо стаянье прорвётся
с концом отчаянья,
Отраженный раскалённый мир
Уведённый зрачком!

А, отвагой лет...
При... камень без бездны —
Во просторах насквозь 3у...
Мне стяжной зовёт й минуту,
Как словный мир...
Прорезая эпохи и казни,
И другие эпохи,

1984

Перед боем

Кони щиплют клевер на завтрашнем поле боя
Полководцы
Мерят циркулями поля — выбирай любое!
Не политы
Муравьиные тропы ещё ни свинцом, ни кровью.
Только утром —
Грянет, и бледный всадник лицо откроет
Перед боем.
Молодые солдаты слушают байки старых
офицеров,
Пишут письма, а после кто-то берёт гитару.
Затихают
К ночи травы на поле боя, и пахнет мёдом.
Только утром —
Грянет, и ~~к~~ завтра будут уже от мёртвых.

1984
ШИЗО

А когда тебя скосит в битвах,
Ты увидишь: люди придут.
На тебя, ещё не зарытого,
Они бросят комья земли.
И друзья, и просто знакомые —
Вон их сколько! и странно розд,
Если брошенные комья
обернутся комьями грязи;
Кто-то робко, а кто-то смело:
— Эка невидаль — за свободу!
Ты победы для них не сделал.
Вот и грязь — от плохой погоды.

1984
ШИЗО

—2—

Если долго идти от автобуса снежной дорогой,
Ориентируясь больше по звёздам, чем по фонарям,
То растает ... на губах незрелой морошкой,
и покажется дым кораблей посреди амбара.
Как оснеженные заборы, поднимемся мы на ступени,
и откроется тёмная дверь под лёгким ключа,
и привыкло шарахнутся в сторону быстрые тени
из комнаты тех, кто ушагал в пустоте по углам.
В кухне кран заскулит по-щенячьи, услышав хозяев,
Заскрипит половица, ругаясь, что поздно пришли,
и маленький месяц, за долгую зиму взяв чуб,
Сунет рожки в окно, как любая зверюшка земли.
Мы стекло разведём, чтоб согрелись к нам добрые люди,
Чтоб звенел и звенел колокольчик у наших дверей...
Если долго идти - это всё обязательно будет
Посреди амбара. Но которого из амбарей?

1985

Наш свод достаточно врочен-
Как холод стеклянной колбы
Наш мир достаточно вечен-
мы равное посеяли оба.
Но всё же мы пишем письма
Кустыми... словами.
Ты разве не знал, Создатель,
Голубушки упрямых,
и хрупких, но гордых плечи,
стыдящихся горбить плечи,
Умеющих с Божьим взглядом
Скрестить глаза человечьи.
Мы будем друг к другу рваться
(ох, береги приборы!)
На все Твои лабиринты
Выдумывая - порох!
На смертную нашу муку-
Слабая слеза победы,
На всё - закусив улыбку,
Без слёз на. С кого бы это..
Не твой ли закон, что слина
Лишь крепче после обжига,
Что если души двое-
трубок неистержим!
В неряшливую голбу
Оглядись - и махни рукой,
Ну что тебе в целом стаде,
Ведь снова отбились - двое?

1985

(маргиналии, вертикально:)
Так разве странно, Создатель,
Что в хаосе разбросанных
Не хватало нас: двоих,
Отпущенных на сквозняк,
мы!

1985

пора включать рубильник,
Так что же ты медлишь, боже?
Ещё можно на ведь унять
Ещё красно боязно порох -
Своих погасить мозгами
Стены, запрокинул слова
В неблагодарный свет.

1985

Что колышемся в ритме прибоя-
только ты и вечно на свете
В небе - чёрное и седое.
А в столетиях - пыль столетий
Что исчезает, но бессмертно.
Погоди, февраль, дай додумать!
Не смяв бережём себе смех и,
Не с мороза венной псадцы!
Скинем шкуры и сменим души
На весенние! Клочья шерсти
Оставил-ся - ни снов недужных,
Ни прошедшего, ни грядущего-
не возьмём в весеннее шествие.
Не снег не просохшей твёрди,
Но раскинутый складкам века,
Ниввал нехудный ветер,
...Я придётся - так пройди ветро!
...А всегда простуди к себе,

Призвание

Сегодня беседую с Богом
Вылепил Микеланджело
Ты видишь, это его рука
над Брестскими пляжами
над морем и горами несёт
и над лакурой дальнего леса,
и - слышишь - уже ... высо-
Торжественная месса!
Сегодня строгую ткань надень
и подставь библейскому ветру.
Смотри, какой невиданный цвет-
первый от сотворения света!
Исполнится всё - лишь пожелай...
Тебе - и резец, и право!
Ликуют тяжёлые колокола,
И рвётся дыхание,
и вечный мала
без черна тебя управа!
Сегодня ты - мастер своих небес.
Назначишь ли путь планетам!
Иди всех чудес - искренне себе -
труднейшее из чудес:
не какие ты выпленишь облака-
знаком и взять над твердью
Так встань перед миром!

1985

(маргиналии, вертикально:)
Прямей!
Ну как,
становишься ли - с бессмертье!

1985

Прошедший день издох и не вернётся
Умерли же принять поминки
о да з знаю будет тысяч дней
тоньше мне чернее чем
Восточней, тем трудней
Брести сквозь них. иди первопроходца!
Но медленнее радости вечеров.
Живой бедой не бла мгновенной мигал
День незгуд стынет кровь ни живой.
Пукай не воск. в край, и век сурек.
Не сумерек холённая миге
Нас возвращают на другую землю,
где с молодой совисал ни прием
Свободу - и расплату за неё.

1985

-3-

Человек со свёрнутым в трубку ковром
Куда-то шагает вечером.
Вот сейчас он скроется за поворот
И уйдёт, никем не замеченный.
И никто не узнает, что там на ковре:
Птицы или олени,
И откуда он взялся на нашем дворе -
Где матери в окнах, а дети - в игре,
Где старушки в кипящем серебре
Держат память при поколенье?
Во дворе, где звенят по именам -
Кто убит, кто жив, кто уехал,
И кого зовёт из чьего окна
Надтреснутая Поэзия!
Мимо стука костяшек за сдвинутым столом
И доцентова автомобиля -
Он проходит, неся на плече рулон
С чуть заметным залихом пыли...
Может, он на этом ковре живёт -
И, найдя подходящее место,
Но-хозяйски велит: - Расстелись, ковёр! -
Предварив заклятьем уместным.
И ковёр развернётся со всем, что на нём:
С этажеркой и клавесином,
И с продавленным креслом,
И лампой с огнём,
И с играющим в кубики сыном.
А быть может, ковёр обучен летать -
И тогда, завершив прогулку,
Он шарахнется вверх, не оставя следа,
Из пустынного переулка.
И блаженно разбавит упругий квадрат
С угольным ветром знакомый кусочек.
А хозяин будет курить до утра,
Наблюдая мерцание города.
А потом потеряется в синеве,
Сбросив ненужное слово.
Чудак - человек,
Чужак - человек -
Чего и ждать от такого?   1985

Лукавый старец, здесь ты не солгал!
Остановить высокое мгновенье
Кам не позволит вечное сомненье -
А может, выше будет перевал?
Ведь наш зенит ещё не наступил.
И дымный запах будущей победы
Тревожит нас, и мы стремимся следом,
По-иному исчисленные сил
Не истинится наша высота
Неузнаваема, пока мгновенье длится:
Наполен Аркольского моста
Прекрасней, чем под Аустерлицем.
И кто посмеет, будто птицу бьют,
Стоп-кадром снять пернатую минуту?
Но счастливы и сами, в свой черёд,
Безудержны в стремлениях и смутах,
Оседла на шаг за завтрашней чертой,
Во всех свершеньях наперёд повинны!
И если время скажет нам, постой -
Пройдём насквозь, плечом его раздвинув.
                        1985

Детям тюремщицы Акимкиной

В этом году – семь тысяч
пятьсот девяносто четвёртом
От сотворенья света –
шёл бесконечный снег.
Небесная твердь утрами
была особенно твёрдой,
и круг, отверженный велик,
смыкался намертво с ней.
...Дело было в России.
В тюрьмах, что ли точнее.
Стране, вошедшей в Россию
поместили лет назад
Она за эту заслугу
орден теперь имеет.
Об этом здесь регулярно
по радио говорят.
И песни поют – про рельсы
с лирическим берёзами.
Поверим на слух: с этапе
не очень-то различишь
Зато здесь растут заборы
и вышки торчат занозами,
и шумянка под ветрами
звучит, как сухой камыш.
Ещё тут ведятся звери:
псы служебной породы.
Без них ни этап, ни лагерь,
и ни одна тюрьма.
Испытанная охрана
всех времён и народов:
Про них уж никто не скажет
что лопают задарма.
А небо над этим краем
утверждено добротно:
Оно не сдвинется с места,
хоть годы в него смотреть.
А если оно замёрзло –
так это закон природы

Приводится в исполненье
В положенном декабре.
шёл снег – четвёртые сутки.
И в карцере мёрз. и бабы,
совсем ещё молодые –
Старшей – двадцать один.
– Начальница, – говорили,
налей кипятку хоть вы,
позволь хоть бы реотузы.
Ведь на полу сидим!
А им ответили – Суки,
ещё чего захотели!
Да я бы вам, дармоедкам,
ни пить ни жрать не дала!
А может, ещё вам видать
валенки да постели!
Да я б вас вовсе держали,
свиней, в чём мать родила!
...ну что ж, они заслужили
ещё не такие речи
Небось не станет начальство
из-за слёд просолят
Зима – так пускай не мёрзнут,
всех не топить ни печи!
На то и ШИЗО, не будут
режим нарушать спят
Они голые – видали
казённые балахоны
Да мало ли им осталось –
дело уже к концу.
Онкуле обвесили
лежат, несмотря на холод
И благодевие мыши
бегают по лицу.
А впрочем, никто не умер.
Вышли, как отсидели.
И некому быть над ними,
калеки – да не с войны!
Кто через десять суток,
Кто – через две недели.
А заступились – некой,
кроме себя, вины.
Пускай отбывают среди
законного наказания,
Да летают на свободе,
А тут и без них...

<!-- средний столбец -->
Найдёшься, кому настроит
Забор, цеха и зданья,
Надёжный – к кому города,
Надёжный – к кому краёт,
Ещё не такие зданья –
лазая победит встретим...
А в общем – то что ведущий
Русское имя родное.
Народу у нас хватает,
сегодня, сейчас, при стене,
Пятисотлетности четвёртой
От Рождества Христова ☩

Девочку!
Что же ты,
что же –
даже и не сидела!

Где ты,
Где же ты зима!
Вьюга, где зимой палядит
Забери в ледянку
мне без тебя странно –
что мы не идёт!
Подымись, мы хотела –
Девочку.

<!-- нижняя левая вставка -->
Испытаем будите их метью
Тюремным голосок –
Акимкина, Ты Сталина!
От меня слагаемый!
Почему мать смылась,
что им родила,
свои лета мятая,
серые мысли!

А что режим не в счёт –
Вам они этого не знают.
Разве голым понимат,
как ни у всех зима? Зато!
там, в карцере, сгибались,
начали ни про не мотаться.
В могиле терпел разум,
Вытаскивай меньший срок,
заплати меньший срок,
безчисленных накопления,
Да летаются на свободе,
А тут и без них!

<!-- правая верхняя часть -->
Песенка

Ты прости, сестрица
и маленький братик,
Что я не сказалась,
не взяла с собой.
За Горелым лесом
стану клюкву брати,
Одна-одинёшенька
сердце успокою.

Стану клюкву брати,
ягоды считати,
забуду кручину –
как и нет на свете.
За Горелым лесом –
нехоженно место:
Запою ль, заплачу –
никто не ответит.

как первая ягода –
что хробынка птиц,
лебединой паре –
на роду разлука,
а за ней вторая –
Ала кровь девичья:
Ехали татары,
стреляли из лука.
А ягоду третью –
Ох не буду трогать,
обойду сторонкой,
чтоб ночью не снилась,
Суженому завтра –
дальняя дорога,
А вернётся, нет ли –
на то Божья милость.

1985, ПКТ

А не любо как-то считать (Единение)

Пространство гулкое высоких потолков,
Уже давно не виданные мной
консерваторских ветренных смычков
Привязана, их тайна за стеной.
Где мысли стреляют,
где странны телеса.
Где, как детей, торжественные свечи
нас бережно берут за подбородки
И застилают пеленою глаза!
Я к вам приду с изученной душой,
С ожогами, невиданными глаззу,
как в синий лес полузабытых сказок,
Где всё всегда кончилось хорошо

1986 ПКТ